OVERCOMING FEAR

"Fear thou not; for I am with thee: be not dismayed; for I am thy God: I will strengthen thee; yea, I will help thee; yea, I will uphold thee with the right hand of my righteousness."

Isaiah 41:10

By
Franklin N. Abazie

Overcoming Fear

COPYRIGHT 2018 BY Franklin N Abazie
ISBN: 978-1-945-1-33-76-3
All right reserved. This book or any portion thereof may not be reproduced or used in any manner whatsoever without the express written permission of the publisher, except for the use of brief quotations in a book review. All Bible quotes are from King James Version and others as noted.

Published by: F N ABAZIE PUBLISHING HOUSE---
a.k.a,
Empowerment Bookstore:

That I may publish with the voice of thanksgiving and tell of all thy wondrous works. **Psalms26:7**

To order additional copies, wholesales or booking: Call the Church office (973-372-7518)
or Empowerment Bookstore Hotline 973-393-8518
Worship address:
343 Sanford Avenue Newark New Jersey 07106
Administrative Head Office address:
33 Schley Street Newark New Jersey 07112
Email:pastorfranknto@yahoo.com
Website www.fnabaziehealingministries.org
Publishing House: www.fnabaziepublishinghouse.org

This book is a production of F N Abazie
Publishing House.

A publication Arms of Miracle of God Ministries 2018
First Edition

CONTENTS

THE MANDATE OF THE COMMISSION...........iv

ARMS OF THE COMMISSION............................v

INTRODUCTION..viii

CHAPTER 1

1. What is Fear? 18

CHAPTER 2

2. Conquering Fear...25

CHAPTER 3

3. Prayer of Salvation...51

CHAPTER 4

4. About the Author..63

THE MANDATE OF THE COMMISSION

"THE MOMENT IS DUE TO IMPACT YOUR WORLD THROUGH THE REVIVAL OF THE HEALING & MIRACLE MINISTRY OF JESUS CHRIST OF NAZARETH.

I AM SENDING YOU TO RESTORE HEALTH UNTO THEE AND I WILL HEAL THEE OF THY WOUNDS, SAID THE LORD OF HOST."

ARMS OF THE COMMISSION

1) F N Abazie Ministries-Miracle of God Ministries (Miracle Chapel Intl)

2) F N Abazie TV Ministries: Global Television Ministry Outreach.

3) F N Abazie Radio Ministries: Radio Broadcasting Outreach.

4) F N Abazie Publishing House: Book Publication.

5) F N Abazie Bible School: also called Word of Healing Bible School (W.O.H.B.S)

6) F N Abazie Evangelistic Ass: Miracle of God Ministries: Global Crusade

7) Empowerment Bookstore: Book distribution.

8) F N Abazie Helping Hands: Meeting the help of the needy world wide

9) F N Abazie Disaster Recovery Mission: Global Disaster Recovery.

10) F N Abazie Prison Ministry: Prison Ministry for all convicts "Second chance"

Some of our ministry arms are waiting the appointed time to commence

FAVOR CONFESSION

Father thank you for making me righteous and accepted through the blood of Jesus Christ. Because of that, I am blessed and highly favored by God. I am the subject of your affection. Your favor surrounds me as a shield, and the first thing that people see around me is your favored shield.

Thank you that I have favor with you and man today. All day long people go out of their way to bless me and help me. I have favor with everyone that I deal with today. Doors that were once closed are now opened for me. I receive preferential treatment, and I have special privileges, I am Gods favored child.

No good thing will he withhold from me. Because of Gods favor my enemies cannot triumph over my life. I have supernatural increase and promotion. I declare restoration to everything that the devil has stolen from my life. I have honor in the midst of my adversaries and an increase in assets, especially in real estate and expansion of territories.

Because I am highly favored by God, I experience great victories, supernatural turnarounds, and miraculous breakthrough in the midst of great impossibilities. I receive recognition, prominence, and honor. Petitions are granted to me even by ungodly authorities. Policies, rules, regulations, and laws are changed and reverse on my behalf.

I win battles that I don't even have to fight, because God fights them for me. This is the day, the set time and the designated moment for me to experience the free favor of God, that profusely and lavishly abound on my behalf in Jesus name. Amen.

INTRODUCTION

I may never get the chance to meet with you face to face. But I am excited to meet you here. I love the power of literature. For the most part, this small book is designed to encourage and motivate you.

It is written, *"Thou shalt not be afraid for the terror by night; nor for the arrow that flieth by day; Nor for the pestilence that walketh in darkness; nor for the destruction that wasteth at noonday."* **Psalms 91:5-6**.

As a believer, we are not supposed to be afraid of anything at all. If you consider with me our root in Christ-- in the order of the lion of Judah. The truth is, nothing is supposed to intimidate us here on earth.

"And God blessed them, and God said unto them, Be fruitful, and multiply, and replenish the earth, and subdue it: and have dominion over the fish of the sea, and over the fowl of the air, and over every living thing that moveth upon the earth." **Genesis 1:28**.

If we must dominate and rule our world, we must live a fearless life, here on earth.

"Now faith is the substance of things hoped for, the evidence of things not seen." **Hebrew11:1**

This small book is a book of faith, designed to encourage and inspire, everyone who have been intimidated by the wicked devil.

"And one of the elders saith unto me, Weep not: behold, the Lion of the tribe of Judah, the Root of David, hath prevailed to open the book, and to loose the seven seals thereof." **Rev5:5**.

Come with me! As revealed by the Holy Ghost, and let's examine how to overcome the Spirit of fear.

HIS DESTINY WAS THE CROSS….

HIS PURPOSE WAS LOVE…..

HIS REASON WAS YOU….

"Shadrach, Meshach, and Abednego, answered and said to the king, O Nebuchadnezzar, we are not careful to answer thee in this matter.

If it be so, our God whom we serve is able to deliver us from the burning fiery furnace, and he will deliver us out of thine hand, O king."

Daniel3:16-17

"For whatsoever is born of God overcometh the world: and this is the victory that overcometh the world, even our faith."

1John5:4

"Father Lord, grant me the serenity to accept the things that I cannot change, the courage to change the things that I can change, and the wisdom to know the difference."

"God grant me the serenity to accept the things I cannot change."

Off course, there are inevitable obstacles, and challenges in life that we just cannot avoid. It is written, *"Be still and know that I am God"* - **Psalms 46:10**

For unless, we depend on God, we will become depressed hoping in man. This serenity prayer is essential for everyone who is afraid of uncertainty, fear, and doubt. It is easy to be focus with an agenda in our life. But I have come to a point in my life, where I must depend on God for everything.

It is written, *"There are many devices in a man's heart; nevertheless the counsel of the Lord, that shall stand."* **Proverb19:21**

We are told, *"For my thoughts are not your thoughts, neither are your ways my ways, saith the Lord. For as the heavens are higher than the earth, so are my ways higher than your ways, and my thoughts than your thoughts."* **Isaiah 55:8-9**

God promised us the peace that surpasses all understanding whenever we bring our worries and concerns to Him in prayer. *"And the peace of God, which transcends all understanding, will guard your hearts and your minds in Christ Jesus"* - **Philippians 4:7**

"The courage to change the things I can"

It takes a healthy fear, which I call courage and assurance from the Holy Spirit to change those things which, we think will never be changed.

"Be strong and courageous. Do not be afraid or terrified because of them, for the LORD your God goes with you; he will never leave you nor forsake you."
- **Deuteronomy 31:6**

"For the Spirit God gave us does not make us timid, but gives us power, love and self-discipline." - **2 Timothy 1:7**

"Trust in the LORD with all your heart and lean not on your own understanding; in all your ways submit to him, and he will make your paths straight."
- **Proverbs 3:5-6**

I encourage you today to take a bold step for the Kingdom of God. Until you tell others about Jesus, your Christianity is incomplete. Until you win souls for the Kingdom of God, you are not wise. We were told that he that wins soul is wise.

"And, the wisdom to know the difference."

In my opinion, it is only through the application of the revealed word of God, that we can know the difference between trial, and affliction. God's wisdom will give you peace, and rest of mind. I pray you indulge and become a beneficiary of this kind of wisdom in your life

If any of anyone lacks wisdom, let him ask God, who gives freely, and liberally to everyone.

It is written, *"If any of you lack wisdom, let him ask of God, that giveth to all men liberally, and upbraideth not; and it shall be given him."* **James 1:5**

"But let him ask in faith, nothing wavering. For he that wavereth is like a wave of the sea driven with the wind and tossed." **James1:6**

"And that from a child thou hast known the holy scriptures, which are able to make thee wise unto salvation through faith which is in Christ Jesus.

All scripture is given by inspiration of God, and is profitable for doctrine, for reproof, for correction, for instruction in righteousness:" **2tim3:15-16**

CHAPTER 1
What is Fear?

"For God hath not given us the spirit of fear; but of power, and of love, and of a sound mind." **2tim1:7**

Wikipedia said-Fear is a feeling induced by perceived danger or threat that occurs in certain types of organisms, which causes a change in metabolic and organ functions and ultimately a change in behavior, such as fleeing, hiding, or freezing from perceived traumatic events. Fear in human beings may occur in response to a specific situation, circumstances, or threat.

The Psychologist said-Fear is a vital response to physical and emotional danger — if we didn't feel it, we couldn't protect ourselves from legitimate threats.

But often we fear situations that are far from life-or-death, and thus hang back for no good reason.

Traumas or bad experiences can trigger a fear response within us that is hard to quell.

Merriam-Webster defined fear as — an unpleasant often strong emotion caused by anticipation or awareness of danger.

"There were they in great fear, where no fear was:..." **Psalms53:5**

As a believer fear has no place in our life. There is a healthy fear for example, the bible declares *"Noah was moved with fear."* Such fear is a good spirit.

"A prudent man foreseeth the evil, and hideth himself: but the simple pass on, and are punished."

For most unbeliever's fear of the unknown, fear of animals and other related fears will always be there to intimidate their health, family, safety, and possessions.

Chapter 1 - What is Fear?

"Be strong and courageous! Do not be afraid and do not panic before them. For the Lord your God will personally go ahead of you. He will neither fail you nor abandon you." - **Deuteronomy 31:6**

"The fear of the Lord is the beginning of wisdom: and the knowledge of the holy is understanding." **Proverb 9:10**

Most of us experience fear in different ways every day. Everyone reacts against fear differently.

Talking about Noah, It is written,

"By faith Noah, being warned of God of things not seen as yet, moved with fear, prepared an ark to the saving of his house; by the which he condemned the world, and became heir of the righteousness which is by faith." **Hebrew 11:7**

What does the above scripture mean?

Noah was afraid of uncertainty, and scared of impending tragedy, he was moved into action Hebrew eleven verse seven says.

Fear is very uncomfortable and crippling. But we need faith in God to overcome and to eliminate it. The act of being fearless doesn't mean eliminating fear by itself. It means to fear God.

It is written, *"The fear of the Lord is the beginning of wisdom: a good understanding have all they that do his commandments: his praise endureth for ever."* **Psalms111:10**

"The fear of the Lord is the beginning of knowledge: but fools despise wisdom and instruction." **Proverb1:7**

"For God hath not given us the spirit of fear; but of power, and of love, and of a sound mind." **2timothy1:7**

The fear of the Lord is an understanding of the Deity, and Sovereignty of God. We are accountable for our motives, thoughts, words, and actions. To fear God is to desire to live in peace with His righteous standards and to honor Him in all that you do. The Bible uses the word fear at least 300 times in reference to God.

Chapter 1 - What is Fear?

Briefly here below are my 7 definition of fears

What is fear?

F............FALSE
E....................EXPERIENCE
A................................APPEARING
R..REAL

F............FACELESS
E....................ENEMY
A................................AFFLICTING
R..REASONING

F............FREQUENTLY
E....................EXPECTED
A................................ADVERSITY
R..REALIZED

F.........FANTACIZED
E..................EXERGERATION
A............................ABOVE
R.................................REALITY

F.........FIERCE
E..................EMOTION
A............................AROUSING
R.................................RESTLESNESS

F.........FACELESS
E..................EXPRESSION
A............................ACKNOWLEDGED
R.................................REPEATEDLY

F.........FAILURE
E..................EXPECTED
A............................AND
R.................................REHEARSED

"There were they in great fear, where no fear was: for God hath scattered the bones of him that encampeth against thee: thou hast put them to shame, because God hath despised them" **Psalms 53:5**.

CHAPTER 2
Conquering fear

"Nay, in all these things we are more than conquerors through him that loved us." **Romans8:37**

Although we live in an era of great insecurity, in a time and a place where our safety and comfort are prioritized in every sphere. We must overcome the spirit of fear.

It is written, *"Thou shalt not be afraid for the terror by night; nor for the arrow that flieth by day; Nor for the pestilence that walketh in darkness; nor for the destruction that wasteth at noonday."* **Psalms91:5-6**

"For God hath not given us the spirit of fear; but of power, and of love, and of a sound mind." **2timothy1:7**

"There were they in great fear, where no fear was: for God hath scattered the bones of him that encampeth against thee: thou hast put them to shame, because God hath despised them." **Psalms53:5**

Fear of the unknown can paralyze anyone from taking a bold step concerning their future.

It is written, *"What time I am afraid, I will trust in thee. In God I will praise his word, in God I have put my trust; I will not fear what flesh can do unto me."* **Psalms56:3-4**

If I must speak the truth, everyone have experienced some kind of fear at some point in our life-- whether it's a gnawing, anxious feeling or a paralyzing phobia. Fear is fear, there is no two ways about it. Fear of police officers, fear of fire out break, fear of airplanes, fear of arm robbers, fear of kidnappers, fear of sickness and diseases, fear of divorce, fear of failure, etc.

It is written, *"Say to them that are of a fearful heart, Be strong, fear not: behold, your God will come with vengeance, even God with a recompence; he will come and save you."* **Isaiah35:4**

Chapter 2 - Conquering Fear

If you truly know God, you will have peace like a river.

"Peace I leave with you; my peace I give you. I do not give to you as the world gives. Do not let your hearts be troubled and do not be afraid." **John14:27**

If you truly know God, you will be bold in everything that you do.

"Have I not commanded you? Be strong and courageous. Do not be afraid; do not be discouraged, for the LORD your God will be with you wherever you go." **Joshua1:9**

If you truly know God, you will ever be settled and never worry.

"Therefore do not worry about tomorrow, for tomorrow will worry about itself. Each day has enough trouble of its own." **Mathew6:34**

God commanded us never to be afraid.

"But now, this is what the LORD says— he who created you, Jacob, he who formed you, Israel: "Do not fear, for I have redeemed you; I have summoned you by name; you are mine." **Isaiah 43:1**

God commanded us to take authority over the work of darkness.

"Even though I walk through the darkest valley, I will fear no evil, for you are with me; your rod and your staff, they comfort me." **Psalms 23:4**

We are assured that He delivered us from fear.

"I sought the LORD, and he answered me; he delivered me from all my fears." **Psalms 34:4**

Knowing God grants peace

"When anxiety was great within me, your consolation brought me joy." **Psalms 94:19**

Chapter 2 - Conquering Fear

"For I am convinced that neither death nor life, neither angels nor demons, neither the present nor the future, nor any powers, neither height nor depth, nor anything else in all creation, will be able to separate us from the love of God that is in Christ Jesus our Lord." **Romans8:38-39**

God is our Defense

"God is our refuge and strength, a very present help in trouble." **Psalms46:1**.

"Yea, the Almighty shall be thy defence, and thou shalt have plenty of silver." **Job22:25**

"But the Lord is my defence; and my God is the rock of my refuge." **Psalms94:22**

"The LORD is my light and my salvation— whom shall I fear? The LORD is the stronghold of my life— of whom shall I be afraid?" **Psalms27:1**

"The LORD is with me; I will not be afraid. What can mere mortals do to me?" **Psalms118:6**

"For the Spirit God gave us does not make us timid, but gives us power, love and self-discipline." **2tim1:7**

God is our Confidence.

"You who fear him, trust in the LORD— he is their help and shield." **Psalms115:11**

"But from everlasting to everlasting the LORD's love is with those who fear him, and his righteousness with their children's children." **Psalm 103:17**

God is for us

"Be strong and courageous. Do not be afraid or terrified because of them, for the LORD your God goes with you; he will never leave you nor forsake you." **Deuteronomy 31:6**

Chapter 2 - Conquering Fear

David also said to Solomon his son, *"Be strong and courageous, and do the work. Do not be afraid or discouraged, for the LORD God, my God, is with you. He will not fail you or forsake you until all the work for the service of the temple of the LORD is finished."* **1 Chronicles 28:20**

"When I am afraid, I put my trust in you. In God, whose word I praise— in God I trust and am not afraid. What can mere mortals do to me?" **Psalm 56:3-4**

"So do not fear, for I am with you; do not be dismayed, for I am your God. I will strengthen you and help you; I will uphold you with my righteous right hand." **Isaiah 41:10**

"For I am the LORD your God who takes hold of your right hand and says to you, Do not fear; I will help you." **Isaiah 41:13**

"Do not be afraid; you will not be put to shame. Do not fear disgrace; you will not be humiliated. You will forget the shame of your youth and remember no more the reproach of your widowhood." **Isaiah 54:4**

"Do not be afraid of those who kill the body but cannot kill the soul. Rather, be afraid of the One who can destroy both soul and body in hell." **Matthew 10:28**

"The Spirit you received does not make you slaves, so that you live in fear again; rather, the Spirit you received brought about your adoption to sonship. And by him we cry, "Abba, Father." **Romans 8:15**

"Be on your guard; stand firm in the faith; be courageous; be strong." **1 Corinthians 16:13**

"There is no fear in love. But perfect love drives out fear, because fear has to do with punishment. The one who fears is not made perfect in love." **1 John 4:18**

Chapter 2 - Conquering Fear

WHAT ARE WE SAYING?

Let me break it down here, the devil uses our fear but God uses our faith. It is written, *"And such as do wickedly against the covenant shall he corrupt by flatteries: but the people that do know their God shall be strong, and do exploits."* **Daniel11:32**

Knowing God is all it takes to overcome fear in life.

"... but the people that do know their God shall be strong, and do exploits." **Daniel11:32**

As long as you live, you will be faced with the challenges of life. There are no two ways about it.

You must be determined to face opposition in life.

"These things I have spoken unto you, that in me ye might have peace. In the world ye shall have tribulation: but be of good cheer; I have overcome the world." **John16:33**

In our life time we must confront opposition, and face trials as long as we live.

"What you do not want, you don't watch."

"What you do not resist has power to remain."

"What you do not confront, you cannot conquer."

I encourage you to confront your fears and watch what will happened next in your life. Jesus is Lord.!

"But thanks be to God, which giveth us the victory through our Lord Jesus Christ. Therefore, my beloved brethren, be ye stedfast, unmoveable, always abounding in the work of the Lord, forasmuch as ye know that your labour is not in vain in the Lord." **1cor15:57-58**

CONDITIONS TO RECEIVE THE HOLY SPIRIT.

It takes the presence of the Holy Spirit to overcome fear in life.

The bible says, *"I will not leave you comfortless: I will come to you."* **John14:18**

"But the Comforter, which is the Holy Ghost, whom the Father will send in my name, he shall teach you all things, and bring all things to your remembrance, whatsoever I have said unto you." **John14:26**

"What shall we then say to these things? If God be for us, who can be against us?" **Romans8:31**

REPENTANCE

Sin makes us guilty and vulnerable to the assault and attack of the devil. We must repent of all our sins, and our wicked ways in life.

BE BAPTIZED

".... be baptized every one of you in the name of Jesus Christ for the remission of sins, and ye shall receive the gift of the Holy Ghost." **Acts2:38**

CONFESS OF YOUR SINS

Although we must confess our sins we must also confess that Jesus is Lord otherwise, we remain subject to the devil attacks.

"If we confess our sins, he is faithful and just to forgive us our sins, and to cleanse us from all unrighteousness." **1John1:9**

ACKNOWLEDGMENT

"Acknowledge that you are a sinner and that Jesus Christ died for your sins." **Rom3:23**.

Chapter 2 - Conquering Fear

CONCLUSION

"For God hath not given us the spirit of fear; but of power, and of love, and of a sound mind." **2timothy1:7**

"Have not I commanded thee? Be strong and of a good courage; be not afraid, neither be thou dismayed: for the Lord thy God is with thee whithersoever thou guest." **Joshua1:9**

"Let us hear the conclusion of the whole matter: Fear God, and keep his commandments: for this is the whole duty of man. For God shall bring every work into judgment, with every secret thing, whether it be good, or whether it be evil." **Eccl12:13-14**

In my own opinion, nothing changes around you, unless there is a change of heart. All we have said will remain a story unless there is a conviction within your heart to obey God's commandment. The mysteries of God is provoked only when you fear God, Obey God, repent of all your unrighteous evil ways and seek the Lord forever more.

We must keep HIS commandments, for his commandment are not grievous the bible says.

The bible says in **eccl: 12:14**, *"For God shall bring every work into judgment, with every secret thing, whether it be good, or whether it be evil."*

If you are a born again Christian; we like to encourage you in your Christian life. If you are not a born again Christian we can help you here receive genuine salvation.

"Therefore if any man be in Christ, he is a new creature: old things are passed away; behold, all things are become new." **2cor5:17**

Now repeat this Prayer after me

Say Lord Jesus, I accept you today, as my Lord and my savior, forgive me of my sins wash me with your blood. Right now, I believe, I am sanctified, I am save, I am free, I am free from the Power of sin to serve the Lord Jesus. Thank you Lord for saving me.

Chapter 2 - Conquering Fear

What must I do to determine my divine visitation?

To determine divine visitation you must be born again. The word says as many as received him, to them gave He power to become the sons of God. Even to them that believe on his name.

To qualify for divine visitation do the following sincerely;

1) Acknowledge that you are a sinner and that He died for you. **Rom3:23**.

2) Repent of your sins. **Acts 3:19, Luke13:5, 2Peter3:9**

3) Believe in your heart that Jesus died for your sin. **Romans10:10**

4) Confess Jesus as the Lord over your life. **Romans10:10, Acts2:21**

I adjure you to watch the Spirit of God bear witness with your Spirit confirming His word with signs following. The word says The Spirit itself beareth witness with our spirit, that we are the children of God. Join a bible believing church or join us on our weekly and Sunday worship services at 343 Sanford Avenue Newark New Jersey 07106.

Chapter 2 - Conquering Fear

WISDOM KEYS

Every Productive Society is a society heading to the top

Millions of Nigerians run away from Nigeria, very few Nigerians stay in Nigeria.

My decision to return Nigeria is the will of God for my life

My short coming in America after 18 years, trained me to be wise, to think, reflect and reason appropriately.

If you train your mind to reason it will train your hands to earn money.

It is absurd to use the money of the heathen to build the kingdom of the living God.

Every Ministry reveals its agenda and goal either at the beginning or at the end. Be careful of your life it is your first Ministry.

The average American mind is conditioned for a continual quest to get new things and (discard the former) and throw away old things.

When I considered well, my BMW jeep became my initial deposit for the work of the ministry in Nigeria

Everyone is waiting for you to change your mind until you change your thinking nothing changes around you.

Multiple academic degrees in other discipline gave me the chance to think, reflect and reason

What so everyone are thinking and reflecting at the moment reveals you to the time and the now factor

All events and intents are the product of precise thought processes, accurate reason every event is designed for a designated timeline

Wisdom is your ability to think, to create and invent. If you can think wise enough you will come out of penury

The distance between you and success is your creative ability to think reason and reflect accurate.

Chapter 2 - Conquering Fear

Success is the result of hard work, commitment resolve and determination learning from past mistakes and failing.

If you organize your mind you have organized your life and destiny.

There is a thin line between success and failure. If you look above and beyond you are on your way to success.

Wealth is your ability to think, power is your ability to reason and success is your ability to be informed.

If you can make use of your mind by thinking and reasoning God will make use of your life and destiny.

Think and Be Great

Reflect, Reason, think and be great

Famous people are born of woman

That you will make it is your intention; that you will survive is your resolve, that you will succeed with changes is your determination, personal efforts and hard work.

No man was born a failure. Lack of vision is the end product of failure.

Working with mental patients encourages and aspire me to be a productive observant and dedicated to my assignment.

Successful people are not magicians, it is the will power combined with hard work, and determination and a resolve to succeed that make them succeed.

In the unequivocal state of the mind, intention is not a location or a position it is the state of the mind.

So many people think that they think. The mind is used to think reflect and reason. You will remain blind with your eye open until you can see with your mind by thinking.

There is no favoritism in accurate and precise calculation

Chapter 2 - Conquering Fear

Although knowledge is power, information is the key and gateway to a great future.

It will take the hand of God to move the hand of man.

With the backing of the great wise God, nothing will disconnect you from your inheritance.

As long as you have wisdom and understanding of God, Satan and evil cannot manipulate your life and destiny.

You have come this far by yourself judgment and decision you have made in the past, now lean and listen to God for another dimension of greatness.

Great people are common people it is extra ordinary effort and the price of sacrifice that produces greatness.

As a mental direct care worker I saw a great pastor and a motivational speaker within myself.

Menial job does not reduce your self-worth, until you resolve to achieve greatness see greatness in all you do; you will never count in your community

The principle of Jesus will solve your gambling and addiction problems

The man of Jesus will lead you into heaven,

Everyone have their self-appraisal and what they think about you. Until you discover yourself other opinion about you will alter the real you.

Supervisors and directors are just a position in the chain of command in a work place. Never allow your supervisor hierarchy to alter your opinion about yourself.

Everyone can come out of debt if they make up their mind.

That I am not a decision maker at work does not diminish my contribution to my world.

Although it appears like it was a poor decision to accept a direct care employment at a psychiatric hospital as I reflect of my nine years of experience, it became apparent that I have learnt and experienced enough for my next assignment.

Self-encouragement and determination is a resolve of the heart.

Chapter 2 - Conquering Fear

If you are determined to make a difference, and do the things that make a difference you will eventually make a difference.

Good things do not come easy

Short cuts will cut your life short.

Those who look ahead move ahead.

Life is all about making an impact. In your life time strive to make an impact in your community.

Make friends and connect with people who are moving ahead of you in life.

If you can look around well you have come a long way in your life, made a lot of difference and realized a lot of success in life.

If you are my old friend, hurry up to reach out to me before I become a stranger to you.

Everything I am blessed with inspirations from God, that change my definition and interpretation of the world around me.

I thought I was stagnant and lonely until I looked around and noticed my children running around and my wife cooking.

At 40 I resigned my Job to seek the Lord forever.

My ministry took a drastic rise to the top when the wisdom of God visited me with knowledge and understanding.

You will be a better person if you understand the characteristics of your personality – your mood swings attitudes and habits.

It is the seed of love you sow into the heart of a child and a woman that you reap in due time.

Love is not selfish, love share everything including the concealed secrets of the mind.

As long as you have a prayer life and a bible; you will never feel lonely, rejected and idle in the race of life.

When good friends disconnect from you, let them go, they might have seen something new in a different direction.

Confidence in yourself and in God is the only way to bring you out of captivity

Never train a child to waste his/her time.

The mind is the greatest assets of a great future.

Chapter 2 - Conquering Fear

You walk by common sense run by principles and fly by instruction.

Those who fly in flight of life fly alone.

Up in the air you are alone. No one can toll you accept the compass of knowledge and information

I have seen a tolling vehicle I have seen a tolling ship I have never seen a tolling airplane.

I exercise my judgment and make a decision every minute of the day.

Decisions are crucial, critical and vital with reference to your future.

So many people wish for a great future. You can only work towards a great future.

Your celebrity status began when you discovered your talent. What are you good at? Work at it with all commitment.

Prayers will sustain you but the wisdom of God will prosper you.

When I met Oyedepo, his teachings changed my perspective, but when I met Ibiyeomie; His teaching changed my perception.

I will be successful in ministry if only I concentrate and focus my energy in the work of the ministry.

It took the late Dr. Vincent Pearle Norman's book to open my mind towards kingdom success.

CHAPTER 3
PRAYER OF SALVATION

I am glad you have read this book all the way from the beginning to this point. All I have said from the beginning will remain a mystery until you commit it into practice.

And before you do so I want you, if you have not given your life to Jesus to do so now. Give your life to Christ. I want you to know the truth! The truth is that Jesus died for your sins and because He died you must be alive and prosperous.

What must I do to determine my salvation?

To be saved we must be born again! The word says as many as received him, to them gave He power to become the sons of God. Even to them that believe on his name.

To qualify for divine visitation do the following sincerely,

1) Acknowledge that you are a sinner and that He died for you. **Rom3:23.**

2) Repent of your sins. **Acts 3:19, Luke13:5, 2Peter3:9**

3) Believe in your heart that Jesus died for your sin. **Romans10:10**

4) Confess Jesus as the Lord over your life. **Romans10:10, Acts2:21**

Now repeat this Prayer after me

Say Lord Jesus, I accept you today, as my Lord and my savior, forgive me of my sins wash me with your blood. Right now, I believe, I am sanctified, I am save, I am free, I am free from the Power of sin to serve the Lord Jesus. Thank you Lord for saving me. Amen.

I adjure you to watch the Spirit of God bear witness with your Spirit confirming His word with signs following. The word says The Spirit itself beareth witness with our spirit, that we are the children of God.

Chapter 3 - Prayer of Salvation

MIRACLE CARE OUTREACH

"...But that the members should have the same care one for another" **1cor12:25**

We are all members of the body of Christ. Jesus commanded us to love our neighbor as ourselves. This includes caring for one another as a member of one body. True love is expressed in caring and giving. The word says for God so Love He gave....

Reach out to someone in need of Jesus, help someone in crisis find Christ. Look out and prove your love to Jesus by caring and inviting your friends and associates to find Jesus the Healer.

Invite your friends to our Home Care Cell Fellowship (Miracle chapel Intl Satellite fellowship) In the USA at 33 Schley Street Newark New Jersey 07112.

If you are in Nigeria—**MIRACLE OF GOD MINISTRIES**

A.K.A"MIRACLE CHAPEL INTL" Mpama –Egbu-Owerri Imo state Nigeria.

(Home Care Cell fellowship Group). We meet every Tuesday at 6:00pm-7:00pm.

LIFE IS NOT ALL ABOUT DURATION BUT ITS ALL ABOUT DONATION

What does the above statement mean?....

"Life consists not in accumulation of material wealth.." **Luke12:15.**

"But it's all about liberality....meaning- what you can give and share with others." **Proverb11:25.**

When you live for others--You live forever- because you out live your generation by the legacy you live behind after you depart into glory to be with the Lord. But when you live to yourself - you are reduced to self—you are easily forgotten when you die and depart in glory.

Permit me to admonish you today to live your life to be a blessing to a soul connected to you today.

Chapter 3 - Prayer of Salvation

I want you to know that so many souls are connected and looking up to you, and through you so many souls will be saved and rescued from destruction. Will you disciple someone today to find Jesus Christ?

"As a genuine Christian; it is your duty to evangelize Jesus Christ to all you meet on your way. Jesus is still in the healing business-Jesus is still doing miracles from time of old to now.

Therefore tell someone about Jesus Christ today, disciple and bring them to Church."

John 1:45 Philip findeth Nathanael....

Please to prove the sincerity of your love for God today; please become a soul winner. The dignity of your Christianity is hidden in your boldness to proclaim and evangelize Jesus Christ to all you meet on your way.

There is a question mark on the integrity of your Christianity until you become a life soul winner. Invite someone to join us worship the Lord Jesus this coming Sunday.

MIRACLE OF GOD MINISTRIES

PILLARS OF THE COMMISSION

We Believe Preach and Practice the following,

1) We believe and preach Salvation to every living human being

2) We believe and preach Repentance and forgiveness of sins

3) We believe and preach the baptism of the Holy Spirit and Spiritual gifts

4) We believe and teach the Prosperity

5) We believe and preach Divine Healing and Miracles (Signs &Wonder)

6) We believe and preach Faith

7) We believe and Proclaim the Power of God (Supernatural)

8) We believe and Proclaim Praise& Worship to God

Chapter 3 - Prayer of Salvation

9) We believe and preach Wisdom

10) We believe and preach Holiness (Consecration)

11) We believe and preach Vision

12) We believe and teach the Word of God

13) We believe and teach Success

14) We believe and practice Prayer

15) We believe and teach Deliverance

This 15 stones form the Pillars of Our Commission.

Become part of this church family and follow this great move of God.

MY HEART FELT PRAYER FOR YOU

It is my vision to spread the word of God in print. It is also my vision for you to come to the knowledge of Christ Jesus.

I desire for you to meet God through one of our books, video or other related materials. I will love to hear of your testimonies and encounter with the Lord Jesus. I love for you to take a few minutes and write me a note below.

REV FRANKLIN N ABAZIE
MIRACLE OF GOD MINISTRIES

33 SCHLEY STREET NEWARK,
NEW JERSEY 07112

OUR WORSHIP ADDRESS
MIRACLE OF GOD MINISTRIES

343 SANFORD AVENUE
NEWARK NEW JERSEY 07106

Chapter 3 - Prayer of Salvation

Now let me Pray for you

Father I thank you for hearing me always. Even now oh God, let us experience you free Spirit of power, sound mind and wisdom. In Jesus Mighty Name. **Amen**.

I like for you to believe in God, for there is nothing God cannot do for us. *"Therefore I say unto you, What things soever ye desire, when ye pray, believe that ye receive them, and ye shall have them."* **Mark 11:24**

I love for you to also develop a prayer life, for there is power in prayer.

"And he spake a parable unto them to this end, that men ought always to pray, and not to faint;" **Luke 18:1**

"And the prayer of faith shall save the sick, and the Lord shall raise him up; and if he have committed sins, they shall be forgiven him. Confess your faults one to another, and pray one for another, that ye may be healed. The effectual fervent prayer of a righteous man availeth much." **James 5:15-16**

I love for you to tell someone about Jesus, for there is power in the gathering of the believer.

"Not forsaking the assembling of ourselves together, as the manner of some is; but exhorting one another: and so much the more, as ye see the day approaching." **Hebrew10:25**

"Go ye therefore, and teach all nations, baptizing them in the name of the Father, and of the Son, and of the Holy Ghost:" **Mathew28:18**.

Finally we must win souls for Jesus. We are admonished, *"The fruit of the righteous is a tree of life; and he that winneth souls is wise."* May you win more souls for the kingdom of God. Amen

Chapter 3 - Prayer of Salvation

FAVOR CONFESSION

Heavenly Father, I thank you for making me righteous and accepted through the blood of Jesus Christ. Because of that, I am blessed and highly favored by you.

I am the object of your affection, fearfully and wonderfully made in your image. Your favor surrounds me as a shield. The first thing the people come into contact with me is your favor shield upon my life.

Thank you Lord today that I have favor with God and with man. Every day henceforth people go out of their way to bless me and favor me. I have favor with everyone that I deal with every day of my life. Opportunities that was once shut down are now open to me.

I receive preferential treatment and I have special privileges, I am Gods favored child. Psalms 84:11 No good thing will he withhold from me as a result of Gods favor upon my life.

My enemies cannot triumph over me. I have supernatural increase and promotion. I declare restoration to everything that the devil has ever stolen from me, in my life time. I have honor in the midst of my adversaries and an increase of asserts especially in real estate and expansion of territories.

I am supernaturally favored by God in a wonderful way. I experience great victories, supernatural turn's arounds, and miraculous breakthrough in the midst of great impossibilities. I receive recognition, prominence, and honor. Petitions are granted to me, even by ungodly authorities. Polices, rules, protocols, regulations, and laws and reversed and amended on my behalf. I win spiritual and physical battles that I don't even have to fight.

My God fights them all for me. This is the day, the set time and the designated moment for me to experience the supernatural free favor of God that profusely and lavishly poured into my life. Amen

CHAPTER 4
ABOUT THE AUTHOR

Rev Franklin N Abazie is the founding and Presiding Pastor of Miracle of God Ministries with headquarters in Newark, New Jersey USA and a branch church in Owerri- Imo State Nigeria. He is following the footsteps of one of his mentors, Oral Roberts (Healing Evangelist) of the blessed memory.

The Lord passed Oral Roberts healing mantle two days before he went to be with the Lord at age 91 into the hand of healing evangelist-Rev Franklin N Abazie in a vision.

In all his services the Power and Presence of God is present to heal all in his audience. He is an ordained man of God with a Healing Ministry reviving the healing and miracle ministry of Jesus Christ of Nazareth.

Pastor Franklin N Abazie, is called by God with a unique mandate:

"THE MOMENT IS DUE TO IMPACT YOUR WORLD THROUGH THE REVIVAL OF THE HEALING & MIRACLE MINISTRY OF JESUS CHRIST OF NAZARETH.
I AM SENDING YOU TO RESTORE HEALTH UNTO THEE AND I WILL HEAL THEE OF THY WOUNDS. SAID THE LORD OF HOST"

He is a gifted ardent Teacher of the word of God who operates also in the office of a Prophet, generating and attracting undeniable signs & wonders, special miracles and healings, with apostolic fireworks of the Holy Ghost.

He is the founding and presiding senior Pastor of this fast growing Healing ministry.

Chapter 4 - About the Author

He has written over 86 inspirational, healing and transforming books covering almost all aspect of divine healing and life. He is happily married and blessed with children.

BOOKS BY REV FRANKLIN N ABAZIE

1) Commanding Abundance
2) The outcome of faith
3) Understanding the secret of prevailing prayers
4) Understanding the secret of the man God uses
5) Activating my due Season
6) Overcoming Divine Verdicts
7) The Outcome of Divine Wisdom
8) Understanding God's Restoration Mandate
9) Walking in the Victory and Authority of the truth
10) Gods Covenant Exemption
11) Destiny Restoration Pillars
12) Provoking Acceptable Praise
13) Understanding Divine Judgment
14) Activating Angelic Re-enforcement
15) Provoking Un-Merited Favor
16) The Benefits of the Speaking faith
17) Understanding Divine Arrangement

18) Understanding Divine Healing
19) The Mystery of Endurance
20) Obeying Divine Instructions
21) Understanding the Voice of God
22) Never give up on Hope
23) The prevailing Power of faith
24) Understanding Divine Prosperity
25) The Reward of Prayer
26) Covenant Keys to Answered Prayers
27) Activating the Forces of Vengeance
28) Put your faith to work
29) Where is your trust?
30) The Audacity of the Blood of Jesus
31) Redeeming Your Days
32) The force of Vision
33) Breaking the shackles of Family Curses
34) Wisdom for Marriage Stability
35) Overcoming prevailing challenges
36) The Prayer solution
37) The power of Prayer
38) The Effective Strategy of Prayer
39) The prayer that works
40) Walking in Forgiveness
41) The power of the grace of God

42) The Power of Persistence
43) Overcoming Divine Verdicts
44) The Audacity of the blood of Jesus.
45) The Prevailing power of the blood of Jesus
46) The benefit of the speaking faith.
47) Fearless faith
48) Redeeming Your Days.
49) The Supernatural Power of Prophecy
50) The companionship of the Holy Spirit
51) Understanding Divine Judgement
52) Understanding Divine Prosperity
53) Dominating Controlling Forces
54) The winners Faith
55) Destiny Restoration Pillars
56) Developing Spiritual Muscles
57) Inexplicable Faith
58) The lifestyle of Prayer
59) Developing a Positive attitude in life.
60) The mystery of Divine Supply
61) Encounter with the Power of God
62) Walking in love
63) Praying in the Spirit
64) How to provoke your testimony

65) Walking in the reality of the Anointing
66) The Reality of new birth
67) The price of freedom
68) The Supernatural power of faith
69) The Intellectual components of Redemption
70) Overcoming Fear
71) Overcoming Prevailing Challenges
72) My Life & Ministry
73) The Mystery of Praise
74) Overcoming the Memories of Divorce
75) The Power of Decision
76) The Joy of Christmas
77) The Prevailing Power of Hope
78) The Power of Discipline
79) The Power of Dedication
80) The Power of Determination
81) The Lifestyle of Praise
82) Dream Big

MIRACLE OF GOD MINISTRIES

NIGERIA CRUSADE 2012

MIRACLE OF GOD MINISTRIES
NIGERIA CRUSADE 2012

MIRACLE OF GOD MINISTRIES

NIGERIA CRUSADE

2012

MIRACLE OF GOD MINISTRIES

NIGERIA CRUSADE

2012

www.ingramcontent.com/pod-product-compliance
Lightning Source LLC
Chambersburg PA
CBHW021450080526
44588CB00009B/779